Motion

by Ellen Lawrence

Consultants:

Suzy Gazlay, MA
Recipient, Presidential Award for Excellence in Science Teaching

Kimberly Brenneman, PhD
National Institute for Early Education Research, Rutgers University, New Brunswick, New Jersey

BEARPORT
PUBLISHING

New York, New York

Credits

Cover, Hermera/Thinkstock; 3, © Coramax/Shutterstock and © graja/Shutterstock; 4–5, © Coramax/Shutterstock, © gorillaimages/ Shutterstock, © Elaine Willcock/Shutterstock, © tawan/Shutterstock, and © Richard Peterson; 6–7, © Coramax/Shutterstock, © Tashatuvango/Shutterstock, and © UltraOrto, S.A./Shutterstock; 8–9, © Coramax/Shutterstock, © S1001/Shutterstock and © Pylj/ Shutterstock; 10–11, © Coramax/Shutterstock, © urfin/Shutterstock, and © DenisNata/Shutterstock; 12–13, © Coramax/Shutterstock, © Alina Cardiae Photography/Shutterstock, © Tatiana Popova/Shutterstock, © jocic/Shutterstock, © STILLFX/Shutterstock, © bonchan/ Shutterstock, and © Richard Peterson; 14–15, © Coramax/Shutterstock, © Nordling/Shutterstock, © vipman/Shutterstock, © John Henkel/ Shutterstock, © ancroft/Shutterstock, © Tatiana Popova/Shutterstock, and © urfin/Shutterstock; 16–17, © Coramax/Shutterstock and © Ruby Tuesday Books; 18–19, © Coramax/Shutterstock, © iymsts/Shutterstock, © sainthorant daniel/Shutterstock, and © Winbjörk/ Shutterstock; 20–21, © Coramax/Shutterstock, © S1001/Shutterstock, © DenisNata/Shutterstock, © jocic/Shutterstock, © STILLFX/ Shutterstock, © ancroft/Shutterstock, © Tatiana Popova/Shutterstock, © Ruby Tuesday Books, © iymsts/Shutterstock, and © sainthorant daniel/Shutterstock; 22, © Kevin Radford/Purestock/Superstock, © Pixtal/Superstock, © Monkey Business Images/Shutterstock, © Tamara Kulikova/Shutterstock, and © Piotr Wawrzyniuk/Shutterstock; 23, © Coramax/Shutterstock, © oliveromg/Shutterstock, © Marcel Jancovic/Shutterstock, © jocic/Shutterstock, © STILLFX/Shutterstock, and © valdis torms/Shutterstock.

Publisher: Kenn Goin
Creative Director: Spencer Brinker
Design: Emma Randall
Photo Researcher: Ruby Tuesday Books Ltd.

Library of Congress Cataloging-in-Publication Data in process at time of publication (2013)
Library of Congress Control Number: 2012049188
ISBN-13: 978-1-61772-739-9 (library binding)

For more information, write to Bearport Publishing Company, Inc., 45 West 21st Street, Suite 3B, New York, New York 10010. Printed in the United States of America.

10 9 8 7 6 5 4 3 2 1

Contents

Let's Investigate Motion

When a baseball flies through the air or a sled zooms down a hill, the objects are in **motion**. You probably make things move and see objects in motion every day. Now it's time to investigate what causes motion like a scientist. Inside this book are lots of fun experiments and cool facts about movement. So grab a notebook, and let's go!

Check It Out!

We see things moving all the time, but what exactly is motion? Let's investigate.

- Find a small ball and place it at the top of some steps.
- Push the ball with your finger so it rolls down the steps.

When the ball moved, its **position** changed.

Before you pushed the ball, its position was at the top of the steps.

Where is the ball now? Describe its position.

You saw the ball roll down the steps, but you also know it moved because it changed position.

So motion is a change in position.

How do pushes make things move?

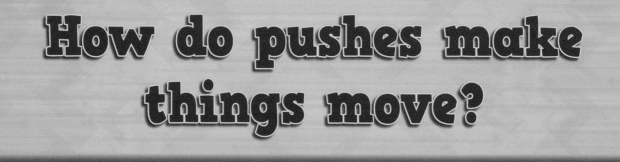

If you carefully place a ball on top of a flat table, the ball will not move. It stays in the same position. If you push the ball with your finger, however, it will move and change position. That's because a push is a type of **force**, and things move because of force. When you roll, throw, or kick a ball, you are using different types of pushes to move it. Let's investigate force and pushes.

You will need:

- Chalk or string
- A small ball
- A notebook and pencil

1 At a park or playground, mark a starting line on the ground with chalk or a piece of string.

2 Stand at the starting line and roll the ball as hard as you can. You have just used the force of a push to move the ball and change its position.

To measure how far the ball traveled, count how many steps it takes to walk from the starting line to the ball. Make sure each step is the same size.

Record the **distance**, or number of steps, in your notebook.

3 Next, get ready to throw the ball.

▸ How far do you think the ball will travel?

Write your **prediction** in your notebook.

Throw the ball and then measure the distance using your steps.

▸ Did the ball travel a longer or shorter distance than when you rolled it?

4 Now prepare to kick the ball.

▸ Do you think the ball will travel a longer or shorter distance than when you rolled or threw it?

Write down your prediction.

Kick the ball and then measure the distance it traveled.

You used three different kinds of pushes to move the ball.

In your notebook, write down what you observed.

▸ Which push made the ball travel farthest—a roll, a throw, or a kick? Why?

▸ Which push moved the ball the shortest distance? Why?

(To learn more about this investigation and find the answers to the questions, see pages 20–21.)

Is a pull a type of force?

A push is one type of force that can move an object. Another type of force is a pull. When you pull a wagon across a playground, you are using force to make the object move and change its position. Sometimes, a push is the best way to make an object move. At other times, however, a pull is best. Let's investigate!

You will need:

- An empty plastic food container
- A piece of string about 30 inches (76 cm) long
- A baseball
- A notebook and pencil

1 Place a container on a table. Make the container move away from you.

▶ How can you do this?

▶ What type of force can you use?

2 Now tie one end of a piece of string around the container.

3 Tie the other end of the string around a baseball. Place the baseball at the edge of the table. Put the container in the center of the table so the string is straight.

▶ Do you think it's possible to move the container without touching it or the string?

4 Get ready to roll the baseball off the edge of the table.

▶ What do you think will happen after you roll the baseball?

Write your prediction in your notebook.

Now gently roll the baseball and see what happens.

In your notebook, record what happened to the container.

▶ Does your prediction match what happened?

▶ What force made the container move?

(To learn more about this investigation and find the answers to the questions, see pages 20–21.)

Can more force make an object move farther?

Forces such as pushes and pulls make objects move. All pushes and pulls aren't the same, though. If you kick a soccer ball gently, it will move a short distance. What happens, though, if you use a lot of force to kick the ball very hard? Let's investigate how far other objects move when different amounts of force are used.

You will need:

- Masking tape
- The lid of a jar
- A measuring tape
- A notebook and pencil

1 Choose a starting point on an area of open floor. Stick a line of masking tape on the floor and place a jar lid on the line.

2 Measure three feet (1 m) from the starting line, and stick another line of masking tape on the floor. Then measure six feet (2 m) from the starting line, and stick another piece of tape on the floor. The floor should look like this:

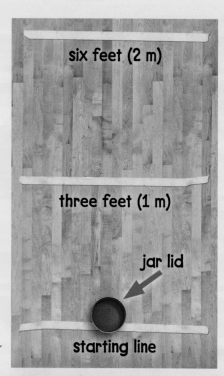

six feet (2 m)

three feet (1 m)

jar lid

starting line

3 You are going to use different types of pushes to move the lid.

- Push 1: push the lid with one finger
- Push 2: hit it with a pencil
- Push 3: gently kick it
- Push 4: push it with two fingers
- Push 5: push it with your whole hand

Predict how far you think each type of push will move the lid.

▶ Do you think any of the pushes will move the lid past the three-foot (1 m) line? How about the six-foot (2 m) line?

Write your predictions in your notebook.

4 Now test your predictions. Push the lid with one finger, and measure how far the lid traveled. Record the measurement in your notebook.

Try the other types of pushes and write down what happens.

▶ Do your predictions match what happened?

Make a record in your notebook of your findings.

▶ Which push moved the lid the shortest distance? Why?

▶ Which push moved the lid farthest? Why?

▶ To move an object a long distance, should you use more or less force?

(To learn more about this investigation and find the answers to the questions, see pages 20–21.)

Does it take more force to move heavy objects?

When you push or pull a wagon, you are using force to make the object move. If the wagon is empty, it's probably very easy to set it in motion. When a friend sits in the wagon, however, it becomes heavier and harder to move. Let's investigate how an object's **weight** makes it easy or difficult to move.

You will need:

- A small toy car
- A cottonball
- A leaf
- A small stone
- A ball
- A drinking straw
- A notebook and pencil
- A measuring tape

1 Line up a toy car, cottonball, leaf, stone, and ball at one end of a table or countertop.

2 You are going to try moving the objects by blowing on them through a straw. A blow is a type of push.

▸ Which object do you think you will move farthest with just one puff? Why?

▸ Which object will be the most difficult to move with just one puff? Why?

Write your predictions in your notebook.

3 Blow through the straw, giving each object one hard puff.

Try to make each puff the same strength.

4 With a measuring tape, measure how far each object moved. Record the distances in your notebook.

▸ Which object traveled farthest? Why?

▸ Which object moved the shortest distance? Why?

▸ Do your predictions match what happened?

▸ Could you have done anything differently to make the heaviest object move farther?

(To learn more about this investigation and find the answers to the questions, see pages 20–21.)

What is friction?

Friction is a force that slows down or stops the movement of objects that are touching each other. When a sled moves down a hill covered in smooth, slippery snow, there is very little friction so the sled moves fast. If the hill is covered with rough grass, however, the grass creates a lot of friction and stops the sled from moving. Let's investigate how different surfaces create different amounts of friction.

You will need:

- Four thick books
- A piece of thick cardboard, about three feet (1 m) long and 12 inches (30 cm) wide
- A toy car
- A measuring tape
- A notebook and pencil
- A bath towel
- Aluminum foil (enough to cover the cardboard)
- Sandpaper (enough to cover the cardboard)
- Tape

 Place four books in a stack about 12 inches (30 cm) high. Lean one end of a piece of cardboard against the books to make a ramp.

 Hold a toy car at the top of the ramp.

▶ What do you think will happen to the car if you let go?

Let go of the car. Measure the distance from the end of the ramp to where the car stopped.

Record the distance in your notebook.

3 Now cover the ramp with a bath towel.

▶ Do you think this surface will create more or less friction than the plain cardboard? Why?

▶ Will the car travel a shorter or longer distance from the end of the ramp?

Predict what you think will happen and write it in your notebook.

Hold the toy car at the top of the ramp and let it go. Measure and record how far it travels.

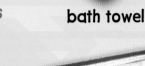

bath towel

aluminum foil

sandpaper

4 Remove the towel. Now cover the ramp in aluminum foil and try the experiment again.

5 Finally, try the experiment with the ramp covered in sandpaper. Use tape to hold the sandpaper in place.

Compare the distances the car traveled on the different surfaces.

▶ Do your predictions match what happened?

▶ Which surface created the most friction? How do you know?

▶ Which created the least? How do you know?

(To learn more about this investigation and find the answers to the questions, see pages 20–21.)

cardboard ramp

Can you use force to make a rocket blast off?

You've discovered that the force of a push or pull can move objects. In this experiment, you will make a mouse-shaped rocket fly into the air by using the force of your hands to create a push of air. Let's blast off!

1 To make the mouse's body, roll half a sheet of paper into a cone and glue it in place. Ask an adult to help you trim the bottom of the cone to give it a straight edge.

2 Using a different-colored sheet of paper, cut out a squiggly tail and two round ears. Glue the tail and ears to the mouse's body.

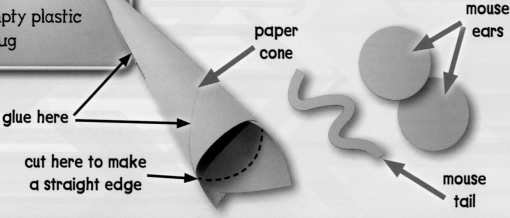

glue here

paper cone

cut here to make a straight edge

mouse ears

mouse tail

mouse rocket

3 Stand a milk jug on a countertop. Place the mouse rocket over the jug's opening.

4 The jug is filled with air. If you place the jug between your hands and hit the sides of the jug, you will push the air out of the bottle.

▸ What do you think the force of the air will do to the mouse rocket?

 5 Let's give it a try! Hit the sides of the jug with your hands as hard as you can.

▸ What happens to the mouse rocket?

6 Try the experiment again. Blow hard into the jug to bring it back to its original shape. Then put the mouse rocket back onto the jug and blast off!

Try laying the jug on its side on a countertop. Slide the mouse rocket over the open end of the jug.

▸ What do you think the mouse rocket will do this time?

Hit the top side of the jug.

▸ What happened?

five, four, three, two, one, blast off!

(To learn more about this investigation and find the answers to the questions, see pages 20–21.)

17

Why do objects fall to the ground?

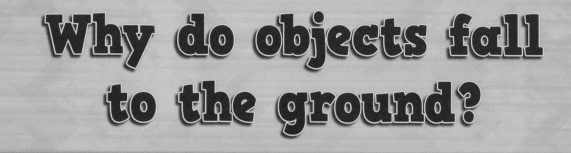

When you blasted your rocket into the air, it quickly fell to the ground. This same thing happens when you throw or kick a ball into the air. Why do objects always fall to the ground? They fall because of a force called **gravity**. This force pulls all things—even you— toward the ground. Let's investigate to find out more.

You will need:

- Two baseballs
- A notebook and pencil
- Two crumpled balls of paper that are the size of baseballs

1 Go outside and hold a baseball in each of your hands with your palms facing down. Then put your arms in front of you so that the balls are the same distance from the ground.

▶ If you drop the baseballs at the same time, do you think they will hit the ground at the same time?

Drop the baseballs.

Record what happened in your notebook.

2 Repeat the experiment with two balls of crumpled paper.

▸ If you drop them at the same time, do you think they will hit the ground at the same time?

Write your prediction in your notebook.

Drop the balls of paper.

▸ Does your prediction match what happened?

3 Hold a baseball in one hand and a ball of paper in the other.

▸ Which object is heavier?

▸ If you drop the baseball and the paper ball at the same time, which one do you think will hit the ground first?

Record your prediction in your notebook.

4 Drop the baseball and the ball of paper at exactly the same time.

▸ Does your prediction match what happened?

You can try the experiment with other objects that do not weigh the same, such as a sneaker and a paper ball.

▸ What happened in each investigation?

Record your results in your notebook.

(To learn more about this investigation and find the answers to the questions, see pages 20–21.)

Discovery Time

It's fun to investigate motion in our world.
Now let's check out all the amazing things we discovered.

Pages 6–7

How do pushes make things move?

Objects move because of forces.

Pushes, such as rolling, throwing, or kicking, are a type of force.

Which push made the ball travel farthest?

You probably used the most force when you kicked the ball.

The more force you use, the farther an object will travel.

Is a pull a type of force?

Did you make the carton move by pushing it?

To move an object away from you, a pushing force is best.

When you rolled the baseball off the table, did the carton move?

As the baseball dropped to the floor, it created a pulling force that moved the carton.

Pages 8–9

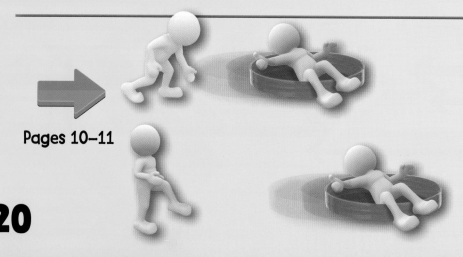

Pages 10–11

Can more force make an object move farther?

A gentle push moves the lid a short distance.

A hard push, such as a kick, moves the lid a longer distance.

This is because a hard push has more force.

The more force that is used, the farther an object will travel.

Using more force will also make an object move faster.

Pages 12–13

heavy
object

light
object

Does it take more force to move heavy objects?

The lightest object moved the farthest.

That's because light objects need less force to move them.

The stone moved the shortest distance because it's heavier than the cotton ball or the leaf, so it needs more force to move it.

Pages 14–15

What is friction?

The car traveled farther and moved faster down the ramp when the ramp had a smooth surface, such as aluminum foil.

That's because smooth surfaces create less friction than rough surfaces.

Rough surfaces, such as sandpaper, create more friction, which causes objects to move slowly and sometimes stop.

Pages 16–17

Can you use force to make a rocket blast off?

By using the force of a push from your hands, you made the air in the milk bottle move.

The force of this moving air pushed the rocket off the bottle.

The more force you use when you hit the bottle, the farther the rocket will travel.

If you lay the bottle on its side, the rocket will blast across the room!

Pages 18–19

Why do objects fall to the ground?

The force of gravity makes all objects fall toward the ground.

When you dropped two baseballs, they hit the ground at the same time.

When you dropped a heavy baseball and a light ball of paper, they still hit the ground at the same time.

It doesn't matter how heavy or how large an object is, it will always fall to the ground at the same speed as other objects because of gravity!

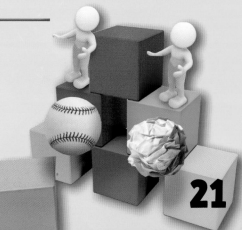

21

Motion in Action

You might not have paid much attention to motion before. Now that you've discovered so many facts about motion and forces, watch out for pushes, pulls, friction, and gravity in action all around you!

1. When you play baseball, you make the ball fly through the air by hitting it with a bat.

▶ **Are you using a push or a pull to make the ball move?**

2. You open doors every day.

▶ **Do you use a push or a pull to open a door?**

3. When you first go to the supermarket, the empty shopping cart is easy to push.

▶ **What do you notice about the cart, though, as it fills up with groceries?**

4. At the playground, you zoom down a slide.

▶ **Do you think a slide creates a little friction or a lot of friction?**

5. Playing on a trampoline is a lot of fun.

▶ **When you bounce up into the air, what always happens? Why?**

Answers:

1. Hitting a ball with a bat makes a ball move by using the force of a push. 2. Some doors you need to push open and others can be opened with both types of forces. Investigate by opening and closing doors in your home. 3. As the cart fills up with groceries, it becomes heavier and harder to push. It takes more force to push or pull a full cart than an empty one. 4. Slides are usually made from smooth, shiny metal or plastic. These materials create very little friction so you can move quickly down the slide. 5. When you bounce up into the air on a trampoline, the force of gravity always pulls you back down toward the ground.

Science Words

distance (DISS-tuhnss) the amount of space between two objects or places

force (FORSS) something that causes movement, such as a pull or push

friction (FRIK-shuhn) the force that is created when two surfaces try to move against each other

gravity (GRAV-uh-tee) the force that pulls things toward Earth and keeps them from drifting into space

motion (MOH-shuhn) a change in position; another word for movement

position (puh-ZISH-uhn) the place where an object is

top

bottom

prediction (pri-DIK-shuhn) a guess that something will happen in a certain way; it is often based on facts a person knows or something a person has observed

weight (WATE) how heavy something is; the amount that something weighs

Index

Read More

Mayer, Lynne. *Newton and Me.* Mount Pleasant, SC: Sylvan Dell (2010).

Royston, Angela. *Forces: Pushes and Pulls (Science Corner).* New York: Rosen (2012).

Twist, Clint. *Force & Motion (Check It Out!).* New York: Bearport (2006).

Learn More Online

To learn more about motion, visit
www.bearportpublishing.com/FundamentalExperiments

About the Author

Ellen Lawrence lives in the United Kingdom. Her favorite books to write are those about nature and animals. In fact, the first book Ellen bought for herself, when she was six years old, was the story of a gorilla named Patty Cake that was born in New York's Central Park Zoo.